INTERNATIONAL COOPERATION in RESEARCH and DEVELOPMENT

An Update to an Inventory of U.S. Government Spending

Supported by the
Office of Science and
Technology Policy

**Science and
Technology
Policy Institute**

CAROLINE S. WAGNER • ALLISON YEZRIL • SCOTT HASSELL

RAND

The research described in this report was conducted by RAND's Science & Technology Policy Institute under contract ENG-9812731.

Library of Congress Cataloging-in-Publication Data

Wagner, Caroline S.
    International cooperation in research and development : an update to an inventory of U.S. Government spending / Caroline S. Wagner, Allison Yezril, Scott Hassell.
        p. cm.
    "MR-1248-OSTP."
    Includes bibliographical references.
    ISBN 0-8330-2925-8
    1. Research—United States—International cooperation. 2. Research—United States—Finance. I. Yezril, Allison. II. Hassell, Scott, 1974– III. Title.

Q180.U5 W3245 2000
338.973'06—dc21

00-045818

RAND is a nonprofit institution that helps improve policy and decision-making through research and analysis. RAND® is a registered trademark. RAND's publications do not necessarily reflect the opinions or policies of its research sponsors.

© Copyright 2001 RAND

Published 2001 by RAND
1700 Main Street, P.O. Box 2138, Santa Monica, CA 90407-2138
1200 South Hayes Street, Arlington, VA 22202-5050
RAND URL: http://www.rand.org/
To order RAND documents or to obtain additional information, contact
Distribution Services: Telephone: (310) 451-7002;
Fax: (310) 451-6915; E-Mail: order@rand.org

This report provides findings from a project conducted by the Science and Technology Policy Institute (S&TPI) at RAND for the White House Office of Science Technology Policy. The White House Office of Science and Technology Policy asked RAND to assess the extent of international research and development (R&D) cooperation and the nature of these activities being sponsored by the U.S. government. This report examines the current state of international collaboration in science and then details the role of the U.S. federal government in participating in this activity, specifically through its funding of mission-oriented and scientific R&D.

This project is part of a series of projects that have resulted in earlier RAND reports, including:

- *International Cooperation in Research and Development: An Inventory of U.S. Government Spending and a Framework for Measuring Benefits*, RAND, MR-900, 1997;

- *International Agreements on Cooperation in Remote Sensing and Earth Observation*, RAND, MR-972, 1998; and

- *U.S. Government Funding of Cooperative Research and Development in North America*, RAND, MR-1115, 1999.[1]

Originally created by Congress in 1991 as the Critical Technologies Institute and renamed in 1998, the Science and Technology Policy Institute is a federally funded research and development center sponsored by the National Science Foundation and managed by RAND. The Institute's mission is to help improve public policy by conducting objective, independent research and analysis on policy issues that involve science and technology. To this end, the Institute

- Supports the Office of Science and Technology Policy and other Executive Branch agencies, offices, and councils

- Helps science and technology decisionmakers understand the likely consequences of their decisions and choose among alternative policies

---

[1]These reports are available on the web at http://www.rand.org/centers/stpi/stp. Paper copies are available from order@rand.org.

- Helps improve understanding in both the public and private sectors of the ways in which science and technology can better serve national objectives.

Science and Technology Policy Institute research focuses on problems of science and technology policy that involve multiple agencies. In carrying out its mission, the Institute consults broadly with representatives from private industry, institutions of higher education, and other nonprofit institutions.

Inquiries regarding the Science and Technology Policy Institute may be directed to the addresses below.

Bruce Don
Director, Science and Technology Policy Institute at RAND
1200 South Hayes Street
Arlington, VA 22202-5050
Phone: (703) 413-1100 x5351
Web: http://www.rand.org/centers/stpi
Email: stpi@rand.org

CONTENTS

FIGURES

TABLES

THE CHANGING INTERNATIONAL CONTEXT FOR INTERNATIONAL COOPERATION IN RESEARCH AND DEVELOPMENT

Developments in science and technology are increasingly the result of international collaboration. Many indicators show increasing links among world scientists to conduct joint research, share data, conduct international meetings, develop common standards, and transfer technology. Data suggest that this activity is not just increasing but is changing the conduct, organization, and outputs of scientific research around the world.

Scientific research is becoming

- More globalized—increasing numbers of countries are building their scientific capabilities and participating in world science;

- More collaborative—a growing proportion of projects and the publications they produce result from collaborations by investigators from a mix of nations; and

- More "distributed"—scientific teams are collaborating across greater distances and involve more widely dispersed expertise.

These shifts challenge the notion of a nationally based science and technology (S&T) policy: national boundaries have diminishing significance for scientific activities, and the results of research are not necessarily exploited at their origin. The U.S. is, on one hand, benefiting from the increasing dynamism of world science; on the other hand, it is more difficult to show direct benefit for dollars spent.

Even as S&T becomes more internationalized, voices within the United States are calling for more rational governance of the U.S. S&T system and a balanced allocation of R&D funds. Furthermore, there is increasing pressure, as exemplified by the Government Performance and Review Act of 1993, to justify public funding of scientific activity and point to measurable benefits from government investments in S&T. These pressures have devolved to the level of the individual scientist, who is often called to account for the outputs and outcomes of his or her research and asked to show benefit of public spending.

The potential conflict between these two developments—the globalization of S&T and the growing demand for rationalizing national S&T policy—raises some critical questions for S&T decisionmaking, including:

- To what extent are the benefits of U.S. investment in S&T accruing to U.S. taxpayers, as opposed to being dispersed around the globe?

- Has the longtime U.S. investment in scientific capacity-building overseas, especially in developing countries, finally succeeded to the point that it has created collaborators (or even competitors) where once it sought mainly to train and assist?

- What does the increased globalization and distributed nature of scientific research and development (R&D) imply for the governance of R&D in the United States?

A key to addressing these questions is understanding the scope and nature of U.S. investment in international scientific cooperation and the relationship between that investment and recent global S&T trends. To aid this process, this report describes and characterizes U.S. government spending on international cooperative research and development (ICRD). Drawing from fiscal year (FY) 1997 data, the report updates an earlier RAND report, and thus begins to lay groundwork for an analysis of recent trends in ICRD and an assessment of the U.S. benefit from investment in international scientific research. The report addresses three questions:

- How much does the U.S. government spend annually on ICRD?

- Who spends the money?

- Where is it being spent?

U.S. SPENDING ON ICRD

The federal government spent approximately $4.4 billion on ICRD in FY97. This amount constitutes about 6 percent of the total federal R&D budget of $72 million. The $4.4 billion total represents a marked increase from the $3.3 billion identified in FY95. It is not clear, however, whether this higher figure corresponds to an actual increase in expenditures. There may be some increase, but just as likely, it reflects an increased awareness of the importance of international S&T and therefore improved reporting from agencies as well as improved knowledge and collection methods on RAND's part.

The U.S. government funds a wide range of research-related activities that involve some form of international cooperation. These include research collaboration, technical support, operational support, conferences, database development, technology transfer, and standards development. The majority of these activities, while international in character, still take place in the United States.

Research collaboration, in which scientists from different countries work together to address a common research problem, accounts for over 90 percent of all U.S.-funded

ICRD. Collaboration takes two forms: binational collaboration between U.S. scientists and those of one other nation; and multinational collaboration, involving participants from more than two countries. A majority of spending on binational collaboration involves U.S. scientists in cooperative projects with Russian scientists: In FY97, $350 million was spent on ICRD projects involving U.S. and Russian scientists. The amount devoted to collaboration with Russia represents a significant increase over FY95. The second-largest amount spent on binational collaboration was $100 million, spent on collaborative projects with Canada. In contrast to binational projects, multinational collaboration is often characterized by large-scale projects such as space-related science, high-energy physics, and environmental studies and projects.

SPENDING BY FIELDS OF SCIENCE

When ICRD spending is categorized by field of science, aerospace science and technology dominated spending in FY97 and represented more than half of the spending by scientific field. A distant second was biomedical science, followed by the engineering sciences, and other life sciences.

AGENCY SUPPORT FOR ICRD

Fourteen agencies and one independent institution (the Smithsonian) devote substantial amounts (more than $1 million each) of federal R&D to international activities. By far the foremost spender is NASA, which spent $3.1 billion on ICRD projects in FY97. NASA, however represents a special case. Many large NASA projects include but are not exclusively devoted to ICRD. Rarely do NASA ICRD funds leave the United States—these projects are multinational activities where other countries contribute equal funding or in-kind equipment to joint activities.

Excluding NASA, the principal funding agencies for ICRD in FY97 were the Department of Defense (DoD) ($263 million), the Department of Health and Human Services ($215 million), and three other agencies that spent approximately $200 million each—the Agency for International Development, the National Science Foundation, and the Department of Energy. Notable in this area was the decrease in spending by the DoD, from about $450 million in FY95. This change may represent difficulties with the data, since DoD did not provide detailed FY97 project-level funding data.

CONCLUSIONS

This report documents an increase between FY95 and FY97 in U.S. spending for ICRD from $3.3 million to $4.4 million. However, we surmise that this result points less to an actual increase in spending and more to improved reporting on the part of U.S. government agencies and better data collection on RAND's part. The only notable change during the time period studied appears to be the substantial increase in cooperative scientific activity with Russia, tied heavily to space-related projects.

We also have reason to believe that many ICRD activities are still undercounted in this inventory. Agencies generally do not report international activities as such—these activities are embedded within mission programs. Likewise, in some fields of science, international cooperation may occur informally, in which case the ICRD figures in this report would also be understated. Moreover, there are a number of international activities with scientific or technical content that are not budgeted as "research and development" and are therefore not counted in this inventory. We estimate these S&T activities to be half again as much spending or perhaps $2 billion as the activities identified in this inventory. These other activities include USDA foreign assistance, scientific data collection by the National Oceanographic and Atmospheric Administration (NOAA), and mapmaking activities by the U.S. Geological Survey.

Notwithstanding these limitations, the data and findings in this report offer a useful profile of U.S. ICRD activities and begin to lay the groundwork for a process of tracking the scope and nature of U.S. ICRD investment.

The authors would like to thank the staff of the Executive Office of the President, Office of Science and Technology Policy (OSTP) for their help and guidance in conducting this research. The project was requested by Dr. Kerri-Ann Jones, former Associate Director for the National Security and International Affairs (NSIA) Division within OSTP and conducted under the guidance of NSIA staff members Deanna Behring (1988–1999) and Gerald Hane (1999–2000).

RAND colleague Nurith Berstein provided valuable research assistance. RAND consultant Linda Staheli aided the project team in thinking about the different types of international collaboration that mark the U.S. relationship with other countries.

The authors also wish to thank the government officials, too numerous to mention here, who worked with us to provide information on U.S. government involvement in research and development activities.

AID	Agency for International Development
CRDF	U.S. Civilian Research and Development Foundation
DED	Department of Education
DoC	Department of Commerce
DoD	Department of Defense
DoE	Department of Energy
DoI	Department of Interior
DoT	Department of Transportation
DVA	Department of Veterans Affairs
EPA	Environmental Protection Agency
GERD	Government Expenditures for Research and Development
HHS	Department of Health and Human Services
ICRD	International cooperation in research and development
ISTC	International Science and Technology Center
NIH	National Institutes of Health
NOAA	National Oceanographic and Atmospheric Administration
NSF	National Science Foundation
OECD	Organization for Economic Cooperation and Development
OSTP	Office of Science and Technology Policy
R&D	research and development
S&T	science and technology
US AID	United States Agency for International Development

USDA	United States Department of Agriculture
USGCRP	United States Global Change Research Program
USGS	U.S. Geological Survey

Chapter One

INTRODUCTION

In 1997, the Science & Technology Policy Institute at RAND assembled the first comprehensive profile of the nature and scope of U.S. government spending on international cooperation in research and development (ICRD).[1] That report documented $3.3 billion of U.S. government research and development (R&D) spending going to support some kind of international cooperation, including "big science" activities, technical assistance and development, conferences, operational support, and other spending. This report updates this information and expands upon the discussion started in the 1997 report.

BACKGROUND: WHAT IS INTERNATIONAL COOPERATION IN SCIENCE AND TECHNOLOGY?

The first recorded case of international collaboration in science involved the extended visit of the mathematician Archimedes (c. 287–212 BC), a native of the Greek colony in Sicily, to the Egyptian city of Alexandria. As a young man, he consulted with Egyptian mathematicians to hone his theories about the law of the lever and the principles of hydrostatics.[2] The history of science has many cases of cross-cultural collaboration where leading minds traveled to foreign universities, where papers were translated and published abroad, and where inventions were carried and adapted to use in other lands. This dissemination of knowledge has advanced science, enhanced techniques, and often affected the course of history.[3]

International cooperation in science and technology (S&T)—where scientists from different countries conduct a joint project or share common data towards a shared research goal—has been growing steadily over the past two decades in ways that are reshaping the face of U.S. science. Collaborative research involves joint projects and shared data. In addition to these activities, ICRD also encompasses international conferences, efforts to build international databases, funds to maintain the operation

---

[1]Caroline S. Wagner, *International Cooperation in Research and Development: An Inventory of U.S. Government Spending and a Framework for Measuring Benefits,"* RAND, MR-900-OSTP, 1997.

[2]Donald Cardwell, *The Norton History of Technology,* New York: W.W. Norton & Company, 1995, p. 24.

[3]The interplay of science and history is described in a number of works, but perhaps none more enjoyable to read than *Connections* by James Burke, New York: Little, Brown, 1997.

of an international laboratory, efforts to set technical standards, and technical assistance or what was once called "development aid" in S&T.

The United States takes an active part in ICRD: U.S.-based scientists publish more internationally coauthored articles than those of any other country, more than thrice over.[4] Nevertheless, the percentage of all scientific projects that this publication represents is actually less than that of other countries, representing about 18 percent of all articles published by U.S. scientists compared to those in the United Kingdom at 30 percent, France at 36 percent, and small countries like Estonia and Lithuania at more than 50 percent.[5] The United States is such a large player in S&T that there is less need to look abroad when seeking a partner. In fact, worldwide, the degree of internationalization is roughly inverse to the size of the scientific enterprise in a particular country, with larger countries being less likely than smaller countries to collaborate internationally. (See Appendix B for more details.) Although international S&T is perhaps more important to other countries, no other country has conducted a review of ICRD spending such as this one.

Dispersed scientific excellence, while one important factor, alone cannot account for the internationalization of S&T. International contacts, while stimulating, can be more costly in terms of time and travel and more cumbersome in terms of cultural and language differences. The increasing facility of communications and travel has contributed to increased ties, but even here, it is difficult to say that this is a primary factor affecting internationalization. There may be changes in the manner in which science is conducted that are having an even more basic and fundamental influence on the internationalization of science.

Motivations for Collaboration

Current ICRD shares some features with historical scientific collaboration: Both seek to share knowledge and leverage discovery through a comingling of knowledge and capability. However, current collaboration is more often motivated by a need to share equipment, to access foreign natural resources, or to serve a corporate, government, or national mission. The scale and scope of some research projects, activities like global climate change or earthquake research, require sharing research efforts, data sets, and equipment.

In addition to sharing resources, there also may be structural reasons for the internationalization of S&T. The advance of knowledge has come to depend on the active collaboration of scientists with specialized skills drawn from a number of research areas. Research on infectious disease control, for example, requires knowledge of immunology and bacteriology as well as the climate and weather of a specific region, the cultural context of disease, and the demographics of affected populations.

---

[4]Data from the National Science Board, *Science and Engineering Indicators—1998*, Arlington, VA: The National Science Foundation, Table 5-52.

[5]*Ibid.*, Table 5-52.

Weaving together these various strands of inquiry to solve problems is a hallmark of ICRD.

Although influenced by different factors than those affecting the internationalization of academic and government-funded science, corporate scientific R&D is also increasingly international. Research shows that international R&D alliances are up more than eightfold since the mid-1980s. In the late 1980s and continuing into the 1990s, joint non-equity R&D agreements became the most important form of partnership for companies. The formation of these strategic technology partnerships has been particularly extensive among high-technology firms in such critical areas as information technology, biotechnology, and new materials.[6]

Governments also have reasons for sponsoring collaboration that go beyond the most efficient or effective conduct of science. These missions include the foreign policy needs of government, economic competitiveness and trade, humanitarian aid, and more broadly, national security. These motivating factors have been in place for many years. However, the extent to which ICRD is helping to meet these goals has been difficult to analyze because of a lack of project-level data. Without this level of detail, ICRD has been characterized as consisting largely of two kinds of activities: (1) "big science" projects involving a number of countries in building and sharing large-scale equipment; and (2) development assistance programs helping developing countries to apply S&T to specific problems.

What is different now, and what this report highlights, is the increasing role of distributed, scientist-to-scientist collaboration, a work among equals, that takes place on an interdisciplinary, team-based level. Project-level data make it possible to examine the nature of these activities, as well as to explore the extent to which this is truly a different kind of scientific collaboration from big science or development assistance. Moreover, such examination makes it possible to craft metrics for this third type of activity, metrics that will be different from the measures that government has used to judge the usefulness of big science and S&T for development.[7]

Even within this third ICRD category of distributed, scientist-to-scientist R&D projects, activities are usually not funded or conducted simply for the sake of sponsoring international activities. While international collaboration is generally viewed favorably by granting institutions, the U.S. government's S&T activities usually meet specific mission requirements or build scientific capabilities central to national interests. Activities like space science, energy research, disease control, and ocean and environmental studies are conducted collaboratively because they help meet the goals of governments or enhance scientific excellence. ICRD is simply, at times, the best way to reach a national goal.

---

[6]Research by John Hagedorn, quoted in John Jankowski, "R&D: Foundation for Innovation," in *Research-Technology Management*, Industrial Research Institute, Vol. 41 No. 2, March–April 1998, p. 18.

[7]A discussion of metrics that could profitably be applied to ICRD can be found in *International Cooperation in Research and Development*, RAND, MR-900-OSTP; see earlier citation.

POLICY QUESTIONS: THE INTERNATIONALIZATION OF SCIENCE AND TECHNOLOGY

The increasingly global and international character of scientific research is raising difficult questions for national investment in S&T. Should nations identify specific areas of S&T for national support when it is uncertain where R&D will be conducted and whether it will be exploited domestically? Is ICRD serving national goals when the knowledge and expertise associated with it are distributed and disbursed world-wide? Does the location of R&D spending have an impact on its use, dissemination, and impact? Can the government be sure that the U.S. taxpayer is benefiting from ICRD? Does the U.S. ICRD portfolio complement or compete with domestic spending?

The decision to sponsor international S&T is at the crux of two tensions within the U.S. R&D policy environment: The first of these is created by the desire for control and rationality. While recent studies call for infusing more balance and a rational priority-setting process into R&D allocation,[8] the complexity of R&D spending and the increasing numbers of global interchanges confound rational organization. The concept of tying public funding more closely to national goals has an intuitive appeal as does the idea of balancing spending across disciplines. At the same time, however, the global, collectivized, interdisciplinary, and distributed practice of science makes it harder to rationalize spending, identify where funds are spent, or track outcomes.

The second tension is created by a desire to ensure that the benefits of public spending are accounted for and accrue directly to taxpayers. The requirements for accountability, recently infused by legislative mandate into science, have devolved to the researchers, as descriptions of outputs and outcomes become part of the requirements of doing science. Yet, the increasingly international nature of science makes it difficult to show how benefit is accruing directly to or within the United States. Efficiency is perhaps being served, but it is harder to demonstrate outcomes when the conduct of R&D is widely distributed.

While, on one hand, ICRD increases the chances that U.S. researchers are leveraging new knowledge created anywhere in the world, it also means that less research may be taking place within U.S. borders. Perhaps only one part of a large, complex project is taking place in the United States, and knowledge created here and elsewhere is combined and shared. Efficiencies are gained by sharing. Nevertheless, to the extent that the tacit knowledge created by research is responsible for regional economic growth, as has been suggested in a number of studies of the Silicon Valley or Route 128 phenomena,[9] the location of R&D may matter. We need to know where research is taking place and decide what kinds of research we want to retain and encourage in the United States.

---

[8]Steven Popper, Caroline Wagner, Donna Fossum, William Stiles, *Setting Priorities and Coordinating Federal R&D Across Fields of Science: A Literature Review*, RAND, DRU-2286-NSF, April 2000.

[9]See for example, Annalee Saxenian, *Regional Advantage: Culture and Competition in Silicon Valley and Route 128*, Cambridge: Harvard University Press, 1994.

At the same time, for at least five decades the United States has taken an active role in S&T assistance programs designed to build and maintain capacity in developing countries. Many strategies have been employed over time and in key countries in South Asia, Africa, and Latin and South America to strengthen research capacity. Activities like training and education, investments in centers of excellence, networking activities, support to scientists and institutions, and data sharing have helped move many of these countries from the role of aid recipient to one of collaborator. Have our capacity-building and S&T aid programs worked so well that now we have collaborators and even competitors where once we sought to build indigenous capacity? Does this mean it is time to revisit out S&T aid programs as well?

The complex system of international S&T is difficult to characterize. But, just as the scientific method seeks to isolate and study particular factors in a complex system, so it is important from a policy perspective to understand the whole and the parts of the global S&T system. If the United States is going to have a rational R&D policymaking process, it is more important than ever to know what input is being derived from ICRD and perhaps what leverage we are gaining or advantage we may be losing by funding ICRD. Being the wellspring of funding and knowledge from which the world draws is a reasonable role for U.S. science, but it should be an explicit one and not simply the result of secondary effects. Moreover, as foreign science grows in capacity, it is important for the United States to know where good science is being done abroad so that this knowledge can be tapped to solve a national problem. Finally, the use of S&T as a tool for development may need redefinition.

Since the earlier RAND report's publication, the progression of current trends has made it both more difficult yet also more important to track U.S. cooperative R&D activities. In order to understand the role of ICRD in benefiting the United States and in supporting global S&T, a number of building blocks must be put in place, including the following:

- How much the United States spends on international cooperation in R&D;

- Which agencies spend it;

- Where the funds are spent; and

- What derives from this spending.

This study answers the first three questions and suggests an approach to the fourth. U.S. government spending on ICRD is worth monitoring on a continuing basis in order to understand these factors and how the United States wants to use ICRD as a tool for U.S. domestic and foreign policy. The 1997 RAND study laid the baseline for understanding how much of the U.S. government's R&D budget was being spent on ICRD; this report begins the process of detailing *trends* in such spending.

ORGANIZATION OF THIS REPORT

The next chapter details U.S. government spending on ICRD. The first appendix details the methodology used to create the data in this report. The second appendix provides data and background on the internationalization of S&T. The third appendix provides data on U.S. government spending on ICRD.

Chapter Two

FINDINGS—U.S. GOVERNMENT SPONSORSHIP OF INTERNATIONAL COOPERATION IN RESEARCH AND DEVELOPMENT

The U.S. federal government spent approximately $4.4 billion on projects involving ICRD in FY97.[1] This amount constitutes about 6 percent of the $72 billion of government R&D spending in that year.[2] This compares positively with findings from an earlier study analyzing FY95 data that identified $3.3 billion in government funding for ICRD. This number may represent a real increase in ICRD between FY95 and FY97. Nevertheless, some of the increase can be attributed to better reporting on the part of agencies as they have become more aware of the importance of tracking and accounting for ICRD activities.

Fourteen government agencies actively supported more than $1 million of ICRD in FY97. Over 110 countries have been reported as partners in or as the location for cooperative research activity. Cooperation spans most areas of S&T but is heavily concentrated in aerospace and aeronautics, biomedical and other life sciences, and engineering.

This chapter presents the results of our data collection and analysis. The analysis focuses on

- the share of ICRD going to multinational and binational activities;

- the character of that spending;

- international partners in binational collaborations;

- fields of science represented in collaborative activities;

- agency-level support for ICRD; and

- mechanisms for conducting ICRD.

---

[1] This includes only one-fourth of the funding appropriated for the International Space Station, even though, in its essential mission, the space station is an international project. However, much of the R&D for the International Space Station is done by U.S. researchers, and including the total $1.9 billion of Station funding skews the final number and misrepresents the extent of international research activities.

[2] All dollar figures are in actual dollars, not constant dollars.

MULTINATIONAL AND BINATIONAL ICRD ACTIVITIES

Multinational cooperation, where researchers from more than two countries work together on a specific project, accounts for $3.6 billion of the $4.4 billion identified as ICRD. Multinational spending dominates ICRD because of the huge financial investments required by big science projects such as fusion research, other high-energy physics activities, the space station, and other aerospace and aeronautics research where large scale equipment is involved. (See the box below on "The Special Case of NASA.")

In addition, multinational efforts are needed to address the data gathering and analysis needs of internationally distributed research efforts such as global climate change and polar research. Global efforts are also focused on ocean drilling. Likewise, health-related research in such areas as the human genome project and infectious disease control have taken on a multinational research character. Some of these activities involve "small science" or distributed efforts, but, since the collaboration is worldwide, these activities have been counted towards multinational efforts. This number also includes global and regional aid projects.

Binational projects account for about $1 billion of FY97 ICRD spending. When binational R&D is tallied, the largest partners are Russia, Canada, the United Kingdom, Germany, and Japan. Funding for binational cooperation with Russia dominates binational spending at more than $390 million.

All parts of the world are represented in binational research, as illustrated in Table 2.1 and Figure 2.1. Countries in Eastern Europe account for the largest regional share, 42 percent, in part because of spending with Russia; Western European partners account for 25 percent; Asian partners account for 7 percent; and all other regions combined account for 3 percent or less of U.S. government funding for binational cooperation.

THE CHARACTER OF ICRD

The U.S. government funds a range of activities that involve some form of international coordination, collaboration, technical support, or other form of international cooperation. Although the U.S. government engages in these many different types of cooperative activities, scientist-to-scientist collaboration is by far the largest single category being funded by U.S. government agencies. Figure 2.2 shows the breakdown by the character of the activity classified for the purposes of this analysis.

This classification identifies the following findings:

- The overwhelming majority of cooperative activities, 90 percent, were judged to be *collaborative* in nature, where U.S. scientists and foreign scientists work together on a common research program, project, or research problem. Funds are spent in the United States, in foreign countries, or in both places.

Table 2.1

Agency Spending on Binational Cooperation, FY97

($000)

Agency	Eastern Europe	Western Europe	North America	East Asia	Africa	Middle East	Oceania	South America	Central America and the Caribbean	South Central Asia	Southeast Asia	Grand Total
NASA	$335,467	$81,436	$37,811	$17,630	$116	$63	$615	$1,294	$239	$145	$127	$474,943
DoD	$16,610	$136,542	$47,031	$16,817	$720	$14,299	$15,331	$600	$1,837	$100	$529	$250,415
NSF	$8,617	$13,621	$11,901	$7,675	$4,288	$994	$5,470	$7,068	$4,325	$2,492	$1,718	$68,169
AID	$1,837		$397		$39,136	$14,196		$835	$2,378	$5,494	$1,924	$66,197
DoE	$42,561	$4,184	$2,690	$5,524	$2,040	$261	$2,077	$825	$230	$409	$95	$60,896
HHS	$1,172	$2,092	$11,093	$2,849	$2,774	$400	$1,693	$1,349	$1,000	$600	$2,795	$27,817
USDA	$320	$140	$4,392	$381	$252	$872	$671	$241	$220	$290		$7,779
DVA	$447	$1,305	$1,905	$84	$629		$303	$0	$7	$4	$168	$4,851
EPA	$389	$165	$2,748	$323					$280	$213		$4,118
DoC	$49	$243	$3,244	$14			$138	$183	$215			$4,086
DoT			$470		$347	$602						$1,419
DED		$1,017	$205	$43								$1,265
DoI	$138	$16	$45				$8		$56			$263
Grand Total	$407,607	$240,762	$123,931	$51,340	$50,301	$31,687	$26,306	$12,394	$10,786	$9,747	$7,357	$972,217

NOTE: See Acronyms List for abbreviations.

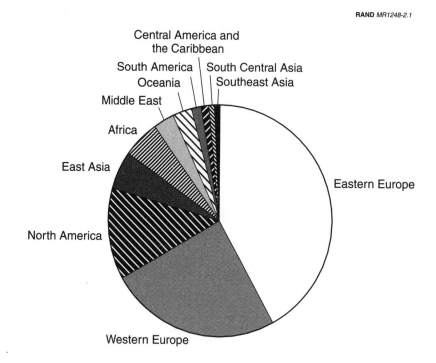

Figure 2.1—All Parts of the World Are Involved in ICRD, FY97

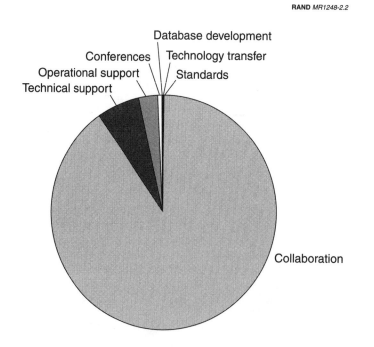

Figure 2.2—Spending by Character of Activity, FY97

- *Technical* support, where the U.S. government funds the application of its own scientific or technical know-how to aid a foreign country with domestic problems or capacity building, was 6 percent of the activities. Much of this funding is spent outside of the United States.

- *Operational* support, where the U.S. support centers of international research, accounted for 3 percent of funds. Much of this funding supports research centers located in the United States.

- *Database development, standards development,* and *conferences* together accounted together for less than 1 percent of funded activities. This set of funds is spent both in the United States and in foreign countries.

Collaborative R&D

Collaborative R&D, where scientists work together on a common research problem or activity, dominates the ICRD projects and spending identified for this inventory. Projects were counted as "collaborative" if they involved scientists working together; they also included cases where U.S.-funded scientists travel to a foreign country to conduct research, even when a specific collaborator is not named in the research abstract.

When collaboration involves a U.S. researcher and a researcher from just one other country, as shown in Figure 2.3, Russia claims the largest amount of funds, followed by Canada, the United Kingdom, Germany, Japan, France, Australia, and Mexico.

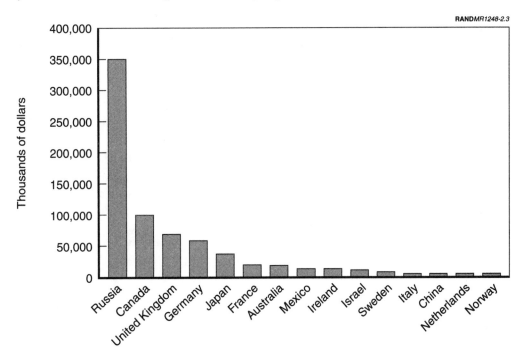

RAND*MR1248-2.3*

Figure 2.3—Binational Collaboration by Country, FY97

Russia

Binational cooperation with Russia has grown significantly since the dissolution of the Soviet Union. More than $390 million was spent on cooperative activities with Russia in FY97, accounting for 292 binational scientific projects. This is more than triple the $100 million identified with Russia in the FY95 ICRD inventory. Multinational projects in which Russia and the United States are involved with other countries would considerably raise this total.

The majority of spending with Russia involves direct scientist-to-scientist collaboration. This is similar to patterns of U.S. cooperation with other countries as well. Of the funds dedicated to collaboration, the majority is devoted to aerospace and aeronautics. The second most common area of collaboration is nuclear energy, followed by earth and environmental sciences. U.S. government agencies most likely to be funding collaboration with Russia are NASA, the Department of Energy (DoE), and the Department of Defense (DoD).

Russia's lead among countries with whom the U.S. government is funding collaborative science is likely due as much to historical and political factors as it is to excellence in science. While Russian science has proved to be world-class in many fields, the United States has interests such as containing nuclear materials and improving the environment in Russia that go beyond links motivated by scientific excellence.

Examples of cooperative R&D activities with Russia are

- Experiments to develop critical space sensors

- Integration of remotely-sensed botanical and structural methods for assessing hydrocarbon exploration, and similar projects in remote sensing of volcanic activity

- A study of Lyme Borreliosis virus as a cause of Lyme disease

- A study of the impact of democratization on Russian families.

In addition to these R&D activities, the U.S. government funds another $20 million in scientific activities with Russia through other funds and programs. Although they are not budgeted as R&D spending and so are not captured in this inventory, they are part of the fabric of the binational S&T relationship. Examples include:

- A project being funded by the National Oceanographic and Atmospheric Administration (NOAA) to retrofit a Russian fishing vessel to conduct fisheries research in the Bering Sea

- Funds being provided by the United States Agency for International Development (US AID) to aid the transition of Russian scientists from weapons to civilian scientific research

- Funds provided under the DoD's Nunn-Lugar Program for cooperative threat reduction

- A National Science Foundation (NSF) special funding arrangement to support the grant-based activities of the U.S. Civilian Research and Development Foundation (CRDF) (see box)

- Operational funds to aid the International Science & Technology Center (ISTC) to provide funds for cooperative scientific research and cooperative threat reduction.

These additional cooperative ventures bring the total spending on the U.S. side for binational cooperative S&T activities with Russia to well over $390 million, far more than with any other single country.

The Civilian Research and Development Foundation

Although the U.S. government's portion of the contribution is not counted as R&D funding, the U.S. Civilian Research and Development Foundation for the Independent States of the Former Soviet Union (CRDF) is supported with U.S. government funds and is responsible for a significant and growing part of the U.S. S&T relationship with Russia. Founded in August 1995, CRDF is a private, nonprofit charitable organization created by the U.S. government as an American response to the declining state of science and engineering in the former Soviet Union (FSU). Funds are provided by the U.S. government as well as by private foundations and other funding sources. The CRDF seeks to foster opportunities for collaborative projects between FSU and U.S. researchers, by encouraging the growth of productive civilian employment opportunities for former FSU defense scientists. (http://www.crdf.org)

Canada

The United States' ICRD relationship with Canada accounts for the second largest share of binational spending behind Russia. In FY97, the total was more than $100 million in cooperative research activities.[3] Our inquiries indicate that informal contacts between U.S. and Canadian scientists may be as large or larger than the formal contacts documented here. Biomedical science, which accounts for 37 percent of the joint projects, is the most common subject of binational collaboration. Earth sciences are the second most common area of cooperative activities, followed by environmental sciences and biotechnology. Ten U.S. government agencies support binational R&D collaboration with Canada. The Department of Health and Human Services (HHS) leads in total dollar amount but in terms of numbers of projects sponsored is third, behind the NSF and the Department of Veterans Affairs (DVA).

---

[3]In a 1999 RAND report, we identified about $60 million in ICRD between Canada and the United States. The increased amount reported here is due to the late reporting by DoD of several FY97 contracts let to cooperative activities involving U.S. and Canadian scientists. Caroline J. Wagner and Nurith Berstein, *U.S. Government Funding of Cooperative Research and Development in North America,* RAND, MR-1115-OSTP.

Other agencies funding ICRD with Canada are DoD, NASA, DoE, and the Department of Commerce (DoC).[4]

United Kingdom

Collaboration with the United Kingdom is clearly one of the most important scientific relationships maintained by the United States. In FY97, the United States and the United Kingdom spent about $71 million on ICRD, a large jump from the approximately $19 million invested in FY95. Share of spending was dominated by DoD ($66 million), DoE ($2.5 million), and NSF ($1 million). (This funding does not reflect spending on S&T under NATO, which would significantly increase the total.) The sharp increase is due to several large defense contracts with UK firms for aircraft R&D, communications engineering and general engineering sciences R&D. Among DoE's projects with the United Kingdom is one focusing on gas-cooled reactor graphite technology. NSF is funding a range of projects including a survey assessing volcanic hazards, biomedical research in malaria and tuberculosis, and research into the fundamental mechanisms governing protein-surface absorption.

Germany

Collaborative projects with Germany totaled $58 million in FY97, increasing from about $15 million in FY95. Spending was dominated by NASA ($36 million), DoD ($18 million), and NSF ($2 million). The sharp increase over FY95 is due to increases in several NASA projects on instrument and component R&D for satellite systems, including the SOFIA program. NASA is also funding with Germany a reflecting telescope that will conduct high spectral and spatial resolution observations spanning the infrared domain and the FAST Mission (Fast Auroral Snapshot Explorer) designed to investigate the plasma physics of the polar auroral phenomena. DoD's ICRD projects with Germany are dominated by contracts in communications engineering and general engineering sciences. NSF's binational collaborative projects with German partners span the spectrum of scientific fields perhaps more fully than for any other countries, and include modeling the wintertime atmospheric circulation in Greenland, a genetics project analyzing the differential effects of facrocycles on RNA and DNA, and an engineering collaboration involving the study of ferroelectric polymers.

Japan

Binational collaboration with Japan increased in FY97 to $36 million from $25 million in FY95. NASA ($17 million) leads other agencies in sponsoring collaborative projects with Japan, followed by DoD ($15 million) and NSF ($3 million). NASA projects in aerospace and aeronautics include the Yohkoh satellite providing high-resolution imaging of solar flares and the Geotail program on geomagnetic tail exploration. DoD sponsored projects including optoelectronic road-mapping and re-

---

[4]*Ibid.,* page 21.

search on ceramic engine components. NSF sponsored a study of the physical properties of galaxies using the SLOAN digital sky survey, as well as projects on gene mapping and microbial evolution.

France

France has increased its presence in binational ICRD by becoming one of the top five binational collaborators identified in this inventory. United States–France binational spending reached $20 million in FY97 from a previous $5 million identified in FY95. DoD dominated spending on collaboration with France at $17 million, NSF accounted for $2 million and DoE for $0.5 million. This increase is due to the initiation of several large DoD contracts. Other DoD projects such as collaborative combustion research aimed at furthering the understanding of the combustion process in gas turbine engines. NSF collaborative projects included research in cell biology, efforts to measure nuclear envelope dynamics in mitosis, a physics project studying particle motion, and a collaborative project on plant genetics. DoE sponsored a significant project on laser research.

Australia

Collaboration with Australia slipped dramatically in FY97 to $19.6 million from $88 million identified in the FY95 inventory. This large decrease can be attributed to the conclusion of several DoD contracts on a shared control and ground station satellite system. DoD continues to fund ICRD spending in collaboration with Australia at $15 million in FY97. Other projects come from NSF ($3 million) and HHS ($475 thousand). Projects being sponsored by NSF are concentrated in astronomy, such as the study of the polar magnetic field of the sun and the mapping of star formations. Collaborative projects with HHS examine the biokinetics of lead in human pregnancies and the effects of maternal depression on child well-being.

Mexico

Funding for cooperation with Mexican scientists and scientific institutions puts Mexico among the top ten countries cooperating with the United States, a step up from its position in the FY95 survey. ICRD with Mexico in FY97 totaled $26 million in projects spanning collaborative research, technical support, conferences, and database development activities. By subject, environmental sciences, biomedical sciences, materials sciences, and engineering are the predominant areas of inquiry for cooperative activities. Together, NSF, HHS, and the United States Department of Agriculture (USDA) account for as much as 70 percent of funds contributed to this relationship.[5]

---

[5] *Ibid.,* page 34.

Fields of Science Represented in Collaborative Research

In FY97, spending on aerospace and aeronautics accounted for more than half of the research dollars committed to a single field of scientific collaboration, as shown in Figure 2.4. A distant second is biomedical sciences, making up 7 percent of all ICRD activities.

The next largest ICRD field identified is engineering sciences, accounting for 5 percent of ICRD activity, followed closely by other life sciences at 4 percent. Physics, atmospheric sciences, oceanography, and energy each represent less than 2 percent of ICRD activity. Figure 2.5 shows how spending on sciences is distributed when aerospace is removed.

AGENCY SUPPORT FOR ICRD

Fourteen agencies and one independent institution dedicate significant portions (more than $1 million each) of their federal R&D budgets to international cooperative activities. A breakdown of all agency-by-agency funding is shown in Figures 2.6 and 2.7.

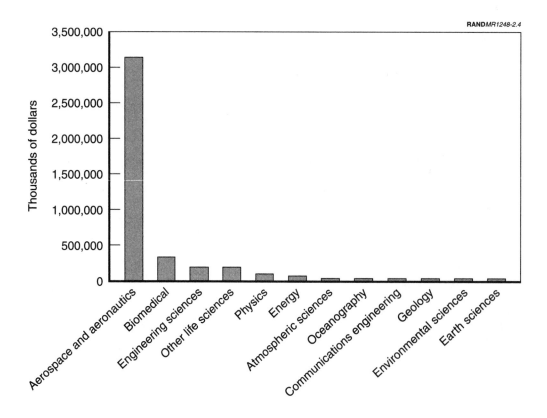

Figure 2.4—Collaboration by Fields of Science, Including Aerospace, FY97

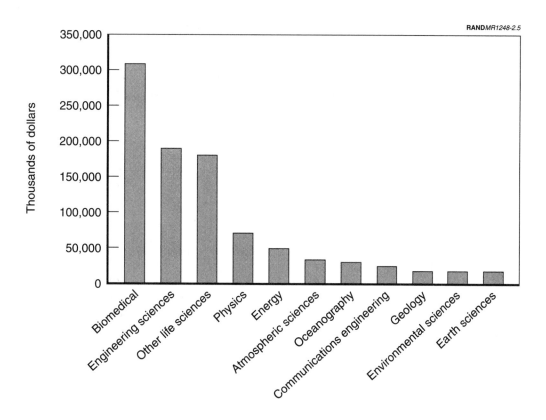

Figure 2.5—Collaboration by Fields of Science, Excluding Aerospace, FY97

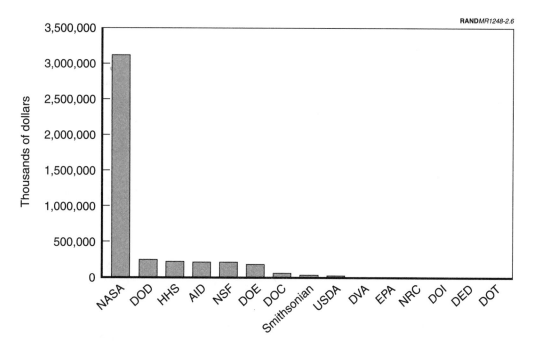

Figure 2.6—Agency ICRD Funding, Including NASA, FY97

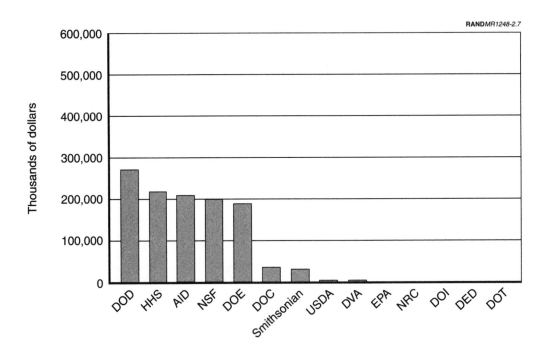

Figure 2.7—Agency ICRD Funding, Excluding NASA, FY97

Department of Defense (DoD)

The DoD devotes a significant amount of funding to ICRD, estimated at $263 million in FY97. This amount decreased significantly from the amount identified in the FY95 inventory, which was above $450 million. The drop is most likely the result of RAND's inability to validate the data: DoD decided to withhold its FY97 project-level funding data. DoD officials claimed that they cannot internally validate the figures. While we were able to get a good deal of data from publicly available data sources, a number of data points for the total estimate for FY97 were reported to RAND as estimates. Accordingly, the figure we are reporting is probably significantly lower than DoD's actual FY97 ICRD spending. Even at the $263 million mark, DoD is one of the top ICRD funding agencies.

Even though the total dollar amount is high compared to that of other agencies, ICRD funding is an exceedingly small percentage of DoD's total FY97 R&D budget of $37.6 billion. The ICRD counted in this inventory was limited to those activities classified by DoD as 6.1–6.3, categories that are roughly equivalent to the Office of Management and Budget's (OMB's) basic and applied research and development categories. The low level of DoD's ICRD intensity may be due largely to the absence of a mandate for DoD to conduct R&D jointly with other countries, in contrast to NASA or the NSF, whose international activities are part of their charter mission.

Based on the funding figures available, the Department of the Air Force leads other DoD units in its commitment to ICRD with $132.4 million. This is in contrast to the FY95 findings, where we documented $240 million of ICRD sponsored by the

Department of the Air Force alone. In the FY97 inventory, we documented $71 million of ICRD spending by the Army, compared to $243 million in FY95. In FY95, we were only able to find $4 million in Navy ICRD spending; in FY97, we documented $36 million, mainly in contract funds.

DoD ICRD spending focuses mostly on engineering sciences ($172 million). This is followed by spending on aerospace and aeronautics research ($28 million), communications engineering ($23 million), other sciences ($7.5 million), biomedical research ($7 million), and other physical sciences ($6.8 million). Examples of ICRD projects include ionospheric modeling; oceanic subduction using tritium-helium dating; the design, development, testing, and evaluation of the fiber-optic magnetic array system; and optical imaging and nonlinear optics.

Department of Health and Human Services (HHS)

Within the Department of Health and Human Services, the National Institutes of Health (NIH) account for a majority of spending on international cooperation. The 23 NIH institutes invested approximately $215 million in ICRD in FY97. Included in this total is the FY97 R&D funding of $26.5 million for the Fogarty International Center for Advanced Study in the Health Sciences to support a range of international cooperative projects, conferences, and educational activities. Among the institutes, the top five ICRD spenders are the National Cancer Institute ($43 million), the National Institute of Allergy and Infectious Diseases ($28 million), the National Heart, Lung & Blood Institute ($13.5 million), the National Institute of Neurological Disorders and Stroke ($13 million), and the National Institute of Child Health & Human Development ($12.7 million). Projects include

- the effects of tuberculosis on HIV infection in Uganda

- investigating the methods to reduce HIV infection in Thailand

- multinational projects on
    - membrane protein modeling
    - new models for the polio virus
    - environmental exposures to the development of cancer
    - the role of heredity in schizophrenia.

The NIH is also host to many international visitors each year. Fellows and visiting researchers make up a considerable part of the international reach of NIH institutes. These activities are funded as part of the operational activities at NIH and are therefore not counted towards the total amount of NIH's ICRD inventory. A full report of these activities is available from NIH's Fogarty Center.

The Special Case of ICRD at NASA

NASA is the U.S. government agency with the greatest dollar investment in ICRD. In 1997, NASA spent approximately $3.1 billion on projects relating to ICRD through its programs in Earth Science, Space Science, Life and Microgravity Science, Aeronautical Research and Technology, academic programs and contracts.[6] The methodology used in this inventory for calculating ICRD spending, when applied to NASA, attributes a disproportionately large amount toward the total when compared to other agencies. Because the inventory counts the full average annual R&D budget of any project where international cooperation is a principle purpose of the research, and because NASA projects are large and often include an international component, the total ICRD funding for NASA looks exceedingly large when compared to the activities of other agencies.

NASA staffers report that they are unable to decouple the domestic R&D spending from the international cooperative R&D spending. Since international cooperation is a charter mission of this agency, each of the projects counted towards this inventory involve a series of joint efforts to supply equipment or services or to share data resulting from specific missions. Activities such as the Space Station,[7] Mars '94, and the Earth Observing Satellite System are funded by Congress with the understanding that these activities will be conducted—and hopefully funds will be leveraged—in cooperation with foreign space agencies and international groups.

In FY97, the Earth Sciences Enterprise, for example, invested $1.3 billion in projects associated with ozone research cooperatively with Canada, stratospheric measurements with Brazil, mapping of the Earth's gravity field with Germany, and remote sensing with India. The Space Science Enterprise contributed $1 billion on projects associated with space satellites including cooperative work with Russia and the European Space Agency, much of which was conducted at the Infrared Space Observatory. The Life and Microgravity Enterprise invested $26 million on the exchange of scientific instruments with France and Germany, remote sensing for research, and control of malaria with Belize, as well as seed experiments with Russia on board the Mir Space Station.

When NASA was working binationally, the projects it sponsored were most likely to be conducted in partnership with Russia, Germany, Canada, and Japan. Multinational projects accounted for approximately $2.6 billion of NASA R&D in FY97.

---

[6]The Space Shuttle program is not counted towards this total because the funds supporting the Shuttle program are not accounted for by NASA as R&D.

[7]It was decided in consultation with NASA that, although the Space Station is an international project, this inventory would count one-fourth of the total spending on the Station toward the ICRD total. This amount represents approximately the extent to which specific activities under this project involve direct collaboration with other countries.

Also within HHS, the Food and Drug Administration (FDA) spent approximately $506,000 on ICRD in conference support and attendance, collaborative research, and standards development activities. This is comprised of (1) $248,000 in Biologics (1 percent of Biologics R&D budget); and (2) $258,000 in National Center for Toxicological Research (NCTR) (approx. 0.8 percent NCTR budget).

Within the HHS, the Centers for Disease Control and Prevention (CDC) also play a part in funding international cooperation in specific areas of health and infectious disease control. In the FY95 inventory, CDC reported close to $15 million in R&D funding dedicated to ICRD. In the course of this inventory, CDC was unable to validate FY97 numbers, so we used the FY95 figure as a placeholder. The agency has continued to be active in ICRD, and, according to press reports, may have even increased its international activities as part of the global efforts on infectious disease control research.

Agency for International Development (US AID)

The U.S. Agency for International Development is the independent government agency that provides economic development and humanitarian assistance to advance U.S. economic and political interests overseas. The agency does not have a scientific mission, although much of its R&D funds go to build scientific and technical infrastructure in foreign countries. Accordingly, US AID's R&D budget is counted in this inventory as "technical assistance" and not collaborative research.

US AID's FY97 budget for international R&D was $225 million. This was allocated among the Global Bureau, the Bureau for Humanitarian Response, and four regional bureaus that focus on Africa, Asia and the Near East, Latin America and the Caribbean, and Europe and the Newly Independent States. The Global Bureau accounted for $140 million of ICRD spending with the bulk focusing on Population, Health, Nutrition ($78.7 million) and Economic Growth and Agricultural Development ($49.8 million).

Among the regional bureaus, the bulk of R&D activities occurred in Africa ($38.1 million). The other bureaus spending internationally focused R&D funds were as follows: Asia and the Near East ($22 million), Latin America and the Caribbean ($2.1 million), Europe and the Newly Independent States ($1.9 million), and the Bureau for Humanitarian Affairs ($0.2 million). As of FY97, US AID's budgets were still highly aggregated—very little detailed project information is available about AID activities—which made it difficult to describe activities in more detail than that available at the bureau level.

US AID's FY97 R&D budget fell by approximately one-third from $313 million to $225 million, with the largest reductions appearing in the budgets for Africa ($34 million), Global ($22 million), and Europe and the New Independent States ($21 million) bureaus. These reductions may have been related to the removal from US AID rolls of countries no longer meeting assistance criteria.

National Science Foundation (NSF)

The National Science Foundation has by far the most varied and extensive support for projects with an international component. While the total amount of funds being spent on projects featuring scientific cooperation, $206 million in FY97, does not approach NASA or DoD levels, the numbers of projects far exceeds that of any other agency. At any one time, NSF is funding as many as 2000 projects that have an international component. In addition to direct research support, NSF funds hundreds of small grants to researchers taking part in technical data exchange or conferences with foreign counterparts. The NSF also funds international collaborative projects such as the Human Frontiers Research Program and basic research components of the international Human Genome Project.

The majority of funding goes towards projects with partners from more than two countries. When scientific projects were conducted with a researcher from just one country, collaborators were most likely to be located in Canada, Mexico, Russia, Japan, Germany, France, India, and the United Kingdom. A portion of funds also supports the maintenance and operations of international centers for research.

Within the NSF directorates, Geosciences leads other directorates in funding projects for international collaborative functions. Geosciences supports large international projects such as ocean drilling, global climate change, and scores of smaller projects on earthquake sciences and seismology. The Directorate on Social, Behavioral & Economic Sciences follows closely behind Geosciences in total commitments to projects with an international component, in large part because this directorate contains the Division on International Cooperative Scientific Activities, a division of NSF providing support to projects that have an international component. Mathematical and Physical Sciences also contributes significantly to ICRD activities as does the Directorate on Biological Sciences.

Department of Energy (DoE)

The DoE has a specific mandate to cooperate internationally in global issues especially in clean and efficient energy systems and basic energy sciences. During FY97, DoE spent $183 million on ICRD on fission, fusion, electricity, renewables, and fossil fuels. This amount represents an increase of more than $10 million of DoE ICRD spending over the amount identified in the FY95 inventory.[8] A majority of this R&D was conducted within 13 of DoE's national laboratories.

Approximately 60 percent of collaboration sponsored by DoE occurs in the scientific research of fission and fusion. In nuclear fission research, DoE has focused international activities on conventional breeder reactors including reactor technology and reprocessing, liquid-metal reactors and high-temperature gas reactors. In addition,

---

[8]In 1999, RAND researched international collaboration in energy research, development, demonstration, and deployment for the President's Committee of Advisors on Science and Technology (PCAST), resulting in a report entitled "Powerful Partnerships: The Federal Role in International Cooperation on Energy Innovation." The White House, Washington, D.C., 1999.

the fission program has added to DoE's collaborative activities by funding reactor safety research with Eastern European countries.

Fusion research took place within the International Thermonuclear Reactor Program, a multinational effort involving researchers from Europe, Japan, Russia, and the United States, a program slated to terminate in FY99. International collaboration in fossil fuels includes

- advanced research on gas turbines and fuel cells involving Argentina, Canada, Guatemala, Mexico, Peru, and the Philippines

- cogeneration research with India and Mexico

- biomass power with India and Mexico.

ICRD in renewable technologies includes rural electrification, small-scale wind diesel hybrids, and photovoltaics.

Department of Commerce (DoC)

In FY97, the Department of Commerce's agencies, the National Institute for Standards and Technology (NIST) and NOAA invested $41.4 million in ICRD activities, a significant increase from FY95 when Commerce reported only $4 million in similar activities. A majority of this amount, about $36 million, comes from NOAA and includes projects on climate and ozone monitoring, metrology, and marine life monitoring. (Note that these may not be new activities; their inclusion here may result from better reporting by NOAA.) Although NIST does not have a direct mission to engage in international collaborative activities, NIST scientists do cooperate with foreign scientists. For FY97, joint research activities, which often involved extended stays by foreign scientists at NIST labs, totaled approximately $5 million. NIST scientists also keep in close contact with counterparts in other countries.

Smithsonian Institution

While the Smithsonian Institution is not a federal government agency, it is the only nongovernmental body to receive a direct appropriation of federal R&D funds. In FY97, the Smithsonian's federal R&D budget was $137 million, an increase of approximately $5 million dollars over FY95. A significant portion of these R&D funds were dedicated to international collaboration. The Smithsonian allocated $31.9 million of its R&D budget to ICRD projects in FY97, a slight increase over the $30 million spent in FY97. A majority of these funds went towards the Institution's science programs, specifically the Smithsonian Tropical Research Institute, headquartered in the Republic of Panama, and international activities sponsored by the National Zoological Park. The Tropical Research Institute has recently expanded its work to include countries in Latin America, Asia, and Africa. These programs include the installation of equipment to monitor changes in biodiversity.

OTHER AGENCIES

Other agencies of government also fund ICRD as it relates to their mission. These include:

The U.S. Department of Agriculture (USDA)

The U.S. Department of Agriculture ICRD projects totalled $10.2 million in fiscal year 1997. These projects were sponsored out of several bureaus that conduct international S&T cooperation as part of their mission. These are:

1. The Agricultural Research Service (ARS), according to their mission statement, conducts research to develop and transfer solutions to agricultural problems of high national priority and provides information access and dissemination to

    *   ensure high-quality, safe food and other agricultural products,

    *   assess the nutritional needs of Americans,

    *   sustain a competitive agricultural economy,

    *   enhance the natural resource base and the environment, and

    *   provide economic opportunities for rural citizens, communities, and society as a whole.

    This includes activities where ARS-funded researchers, both inside and outside government laboratories, coordinate and collaborate with overseas counterparts.

2. The Foreign Agricultural Service (FAS) of the USDA works to improve foreign market access for U.S. products. FAS operates programs designed to build new markets and improve the competitive position of U.S. agriculture in the global marketplace.

3. The Forest Service office of International Programs offers technical assistance and disaster relief coordination to counterparts in different countries. The focus of this bureau's work is on key natural resource problems and issues in countries with significant forest resources and important forest-related trade with the U.S. Projects include watershed restoration, forest pest studies and forest ecosystem analysis. Partners include China, Brazil, Russia, and Indonesia.

The Department of Veterans Affairs (DVA)

The Department of Veterans Affairs funds research that looks worldwide for solutions to medical problems experienced by American veterans. This includes as much as $6.7 million dollars of research with some international links in FY97. Within this, considerable work was done in collaboration with researchers in Canada, particularly in the area of prosthetics and medical devices.

Environmental Protection Agency (EPA)

The Environmental Protection Agency's mission is to protect human health and safeguard the natural environment. While the EPA has significant scientific and technical capabilities, the Office of Research & Development (ORD) is responsible for the R&D needs of the agency's operating programs as well as the conduct of its integrated R&D programs. The ORD focuses on the advancement of basic peer-reviewed scientific research as well as partnerships with scientists in the academic community. The ORD helps provide sound environmental research for effective policy and regulatory decisionmaking. In FY97, the ORD's involvement in ICRD amounted to approximately $6 million and spanned a wide range of activities including joint watershed management, health impacts of air pollution, and participation in international programs. In addition, the EPA dedicated more than $14 million to research related to the Global Climate Change Program, bringing the EPA's total to $21 million—about what was identified in the FY95 inventory. (See box on page 27.)

Nuclear Regulatory Commission (NRC)

The Nuclear Regulatory Commission contributed as much as $6 million to ICRD in FY97. A significant portion of the NRC's international R&D activities were focused on highly leveraged domestic-led and foreign-led R&D projects, most of which could not be maintained without funds provided by international partners and foreign facilities. The NRC's FY97 R&D program also included two programs for analytical code assessment with foreign country participation and cost-sharing. Foreign participation in these domestic programs increases available technical information and promotes greater dissemination of knowledge and improved safety analysis worldwide. These two domestic programs focus on severe accident research and thermal-hydraulic code application and maintenance.

Department of the Interior (DoI)

The Department of the Interior's charter includes a mission to protect, provide access to, and manage the nation's natural and cultural heritage and advance scientific research and monitoring to improve understanding of natural and human systems. In 1996, DoI consolidated the majority of its R&D activities within the U.S. Geological Survey (USGS).

In the aggregate, DoI devoted roughly $2.8 million to ICRD in FY97. This work was primarily performed by the USGS's Biological Resources Division (BRD), the Minerals Management Service (MMS), and the National Park Service (NPS).

MECHANISMS FOR CONDUCTING ICRD

The majority of government-funded R&D—between 50 and 90 percent depending upon the agency—is performed under government contract or grant and takes place in nongovernment laboratories located at universities or within the private sector.

Other parties conducting, supporting, or promoting ICRD operate within government agencies, such as US AID, or government laboratories, such as NIH labs.

ICRD is funded in six ways: (1) through government-based programmatic activities, such as research within NASA labs that support an international program; (2) through awards—contracts, grants, and cooperative agreements—provided directly by a U.S. government agency, such as NSF research grants; (3) by funding and maintaining the operation of centers for international research, such as the Smithsonian tropical research center or NSF's atmospheric lab; (4) through allocation of funds provided to an independent body, such as the U.S.-Mexico Science and Technology Foundation; (5) through funds provided or reimbursed by foreign countries, such as funds provided to participate in a USGS project or funds paid to the CDC to conduct infectious disease testing side by side with African research scientists; and (6) funds paid in remission of debt held by the United States, such as the P.L. 480 funds available for USDA research with India.

The way in which the government funds ICRD reflects the nature of the benefit that the government expects to receive from the activity. For example, contracts issued for R&D to be conducted in foreign countries usually have a statement of work requiring deliverables that are needed by the contracting agency to meet a specific, program-related mission. Grants are provided by government agencies to strengthen specific areas of science or to fund innovative research that would not otherwise be conducted. In this case, the government expects a general increase of knowledge but not necessarily a specific product. Funds provided to research centers often seek to access specific foreign research opportunities or resources where that resource is not available to researchers in the United States.

The U.S. Global Change Research Program (USGCRP)

The USGCRP was established in 1989. The program coordinates the research and policy development interests of roughly one dozen federal agencies and the executive branch. Its efforts focus on the scientific study of how the Earth's systems respond to natural and human-induced changes and how this knowledge can be used to reduce the vulnerabilities of human and ecological systems to such change. Specifically, the USGCRP research portfolio pursues scientific research on key global change issues, including seasonal to interannual climate variability; climate change over decades to centuries; changes in ozone, ultraviolet radiation, and atmospheric chemistry; and changes in land cover and in terrestrial and aquatic ecosystems. Given the global nature of this issue, the USGCRP also works to develop tools and capabilities to communicate knowledge and improve understanding of these issues. In addition, the USGCRP coordinates U.S. activities with other related national and international research programs such as the World Climate Research Programme, the International Geosphere-Biosphere Programme, and the International Human Dimensions Programme.

In FY97, the total USGCRP budget was $1.8 billion, an increase of $1 million from FY95. The "scientific research" component of the USGCRP portfolio amounted to $688 million, which supported individual investigators and small groups. These activities were funded by NASA ($240 million), NSF ($164 million), DoE ($112 million), the Department of Commerce's NOAA and NIST ($60 million), USDA ($57 million), the Department of the Interior ($29 million), and the EPA ($14 million). HHS, the Smithsonian Institution, and the Tennessee Valley Authority (TVA) also provided a total of $12 million. The remaining $1.1 billion in USGCRP activities were focused on "space-based observation," namely NASA's Mission to Planet Earth, which provides data on the global environment.

CONCLUSION

This report documents an increase in FY97 ICRD spending within most agencies over that reported in FY95 and includes new agencies and additional details about activities with different countries. While the goal of this project has been to begin a tracking process to see where increases and decreases in ICRD may become apparent over time, the project also increased the number of agencies where we were able to document activities. Some of the increase in ICRD documented here results from better reporting on the part of agencies and a better knowledge base and collection methods on RAND's part. It is unclear how much of the increase is due to better reporting and how much is due to a true increase in ICRD, but the result is a fuller picture of government activities.

In a number of cases, particularly in aeronautics and aerospace research and some parts of defense and environmental research, it is difficult to say where national research activities end and international cooperative activities begin. While we have a clear definition of how to determine ICRD (see Appendix A), agency officials working on specific projects had difficulty decoupling international from national activities in a number of cases. This is particularly true in big science projects like space and energy research, where one of the goals of the activities is to share information and equipment. Within these activities, a number of projects take place solely in the United States, but the extent to which these should then be counted as part of ICRD is very difficult to determine.

Finally, this report documents activities where the project or program description specifically states that international collaboration is a goal of the project. In some agencies, the inclusion of plans to conduct cooperative R&D is a plus that aids in the award of funds. In other agencies, mentioning international cooperation may be detrimental and can lead to increased scrutiny of a proposal or project. Likewise, in some fields of science, international cooperation on an informal basis is the rule rather than the exception—in these cases, ICRD may be understated.

Despite these caveats and concerns, these data provide a useful insight into the extent to which the U.S. government is funding international cooperation in R&D. As international cooperation in science becomes more prominent, efforts to track U.S. government funding from the bottom up, while at the same time working to improve the data available on ICRD activities, will remain a crucial feature of public policy decisionmaking.

Strengths and Limitations of This Approach

The data-collection technique used in this study has significant strengths. First, the data are actual numbers. Unlike "indicators" such as bibliometric citations, patent data, and co-word analysis, which are indirect measures, this inventory counts actual dollar commitments. Moreover, unlike efforts that have asked agencies for an estimate of activities, these data have been gathered from actual activities and have been counted from the "bottom up," identifying activities at the lowest available levels and aggregating into programs, bureaus, and agencies. Third, this approach enabled consistent screening of the data using a single filter. This helped ensure the comparability of data across agencies. Fourth, this approach has the advantage of identifying cooperative activities in actual operation as opposed to cooperation proposed in international bilateral and multilateral cooperative agreements. Fifth, the method we used is transparent and reproducible. This allows trend analysis over time and across agencies.[9]

The approach used to conduct this inventory also has limitations. Some agencies do not compile or report data on activities at the project or award level. In these cases, the inventory includes program-based activities at higher aggregations such as budget line items. The implications of this lack of detail for the full inventory is that the compiled data do not reflect the full spectrum of all project-level activities being funded by the U.S. government. US AID, for example, reports data only at the budget line item level, so no additional analysis or comparison of US AID activities is

---

[9]This is also the reason we used R&D instead of the larger set of activities that would be represented by the term "science and technology."

possible. The US AID budget line-item data are delineated by region, but that is the most detailed data we could find for US AID activities. Similarly, the EPA also does not report detailed project-level activities. The DoD provides details about grant-based project-level activities but does not provide funding amounts for these activities. Some DoE and DoD lab-based activities also are not captured in this inventory.

This effort also presents input data only. While this is the first time that a measure of this input has been taken, it does leave unanswered the question of the output and outcomes of these activities. Ultimately, when assessing the usefulness of ICRD spending, it will be important to be able to measure outcomes. Generally, outcomes are also measured by counting indicators such as papers published, patents issued, and so on. Using project-level data, as we have done here, offers the possibility of going back to the principal investigators and asking directly about outcomes. This will help make measurement more effective over the long run, although it will be a significant effort to make such a measurement.

METHODOLOGY FOR DATA COLLECTION AND ANALYSIS

This study examines U.S. federal government spending on international cooperation in research and development (ICRD)[1] in fiscal year 1997. Because of the diversity and range of the ICRD activities being studied, analytic boundaries have been drawn for the purpose of conducting this study, focusing on:

- actual cooperative activities rather than international agreements to cooperate;

- research and development budget obligations rather than the less clearly defined category of "science and technology";

- government records documenting award and project activities rather than reports from various agencies; and

- the creation of a transparent and reproducible approach to assessment, rather than anecdotes of success.

ACTUAL RESEARCH AND DEVELOPMENT ACTIVITIES VERSUS INTERNATIONAL SCIENCE AND TECHNOLOGY AGREEMENTS

International S&T agreements (ISTAs) can be an important indicator of national interest to cooperate in R&D, but they do not provide a count of ICRD. In fiscal year 1997, the U.S. government had 31 active "umbrella" or "framework" ISTAs signed at the White House level. These agreements provide the protocol for sharing scientific data and equipment, exchanging researchers, and conducting collaborative projects.

It has been widely assumed that ISTAs constitute the scope of U.S. government ICRD activities. In fact, ISTAs are nonfunded, diplomatic-level agreements that have no associated budget authority. Many ISTAs are never fully implemented because of lack of funds from one or more parties. On the other end of the spectrum, individual investigators often collaborate with their international peers without reference to the existence of an ISTA. Relying on the list of ISTAs can actually be misleading when the

---

[1]Research and development is a budget term used by the OMB and applied within government agencies to define a specific form of federal investment activity. In fiscal year 1995, this activity amounted to approximately $70 billion. Only those activities classified by federal agencies as R&D are included in this inventory. We recognize that projects and activities outside of the defined set of R&D projects might be considered to be scientific or technical in nature, but to ensure consistency we do not include these activities in this inventory.

goal is identifying the range and character of ICRD actually being funded by the U.S. government. Accordingly, this study identifies federally funded ICRD projects regardless of whether they were sponsored by or were otherwise a part of a government-to-government ISTA.

RESEARCH AND DEVELOPMENT VERSUS SCIENCE AND TECHNOLOGY

The scope of this study is limited to the conduct of research and development (R&D). Although the terms "science and technology" and "research and development" are sometimes used interchangeably, within the U.S. federal government budget system, these terms have very different meanings. R&D is a specifically defined budget category, constituting $70-plus billion of U.S. government discretionary spending.

The OMB defines R&D activities within the federal budget in Circular A-11 as activities falling within these general guidelines:

- Basic research—systematic study to gain knowledge or understanding of the fundamental aspects of phenomena and of observable facts without specific applications toward processes or products in mind.

- Applied research—systematic study directed toward greater knowledge or understanding necessary to determine the means by which a recognized and specific need may be met.

- Development—application of knowledge toward the production of useful materials, devices, and systems, or methods, including design, development, and improvement of prototypes and new processes to meet specific requirements.

OMB allows individual agencies some latitude in determining which activities constitute the conduct of R&D. Each agency may use its traditional, historic definitions of R&D when reporting R&D activities to OMB. As a result, each federal agency defines the "stages" (basic, applied, and development) of R&D in the context of its particular mission. This results in variations among the agencies as to what constitutes basic and applied research and development.

Agency variations result in R&D data that are often difficult to compare. The OMB definitions of R&D specifically exclude the training of scientific and technical personnel. However, the support of research assistantships for Ph.D. dissertation research is sometimes included in the "conduct of R&D" as a grant provided by an agency to a scientific researcher. Moreover, R&D data may differ across agencies in the accounting for salaries and indirect costs: These may be included or excluded from the total R&D budget, depending upon the nature of the research or the vehicle for its funding.

Among the agencies, DoD has the most unique approach to accounting for R&D. DoD reports seven stages of R&D to OMB: DoD budget categories 6.1–6.3 correlate with the OMB definitions for basic, applied, and development R&D—DoD refers to all three categories as "S&T." DoD delineates budget categories 6.4–6.7 as testing, evaluation, and design activities—DoD refers to these four categories as "R&D." The federal government's $70-plus billion R&D budget comprises budgets for all seven DoD 6.1–6.7 activities'.

Specifically not counted as R&D within the U.S. government budget is spending such as:

- endowments, such as the U.S.–Israel Science and Technology Commission

- capital investment, such as the Global Seismographic Network

- operation of equipment, such as operation of the Space Shuttle

- product testing, such as metrology

- quality control, mapping, collection of general-purpose statistics, experimental production, routine monitoring and evaluation of an operational program

- the training of scientific and technical personnel.

Some of these might be considered scientific activities by a reasonable observer and may involve some international cooperative activities, such as collecting, tracking, and reporting weather data. Nevertheless, these activities are not budgeted as R&D, so it is difficult to compare them across agencies or track them from year to year.

The particularities of federal budgeting terms and practices have important implications for this study. To create an inventory of international R&D spending that is comparable across agencies and over time, this project used government R&D budget dollars because these are identifiable, comparable, and traceable data.[2] When we discuss "S&T" activities, this is meant to imply R&D plus other nonquantifiable government activities that support science. Figure A.1 illustrates how the terms are used and where this study has focused its efforts. Figure A.1 also shows how, in an effort to make the data comparable across agencies, we eliminated the DoD 6.4–6.7 data from this inventory, since these activities generally involve testing and evaluation activities not conducted under R&D budgets in other agencies.

INTERNATIONAL R&D DATA IS NOT A BUDGET CATEGORY

International R&D cooperation is not budgeted as a separate category, nor is it reported to OMB or Congress as a separate activity. ICRD activities vary by agency mission, by country, by topic, and by many other variables. Conducting an inventory of ICRD requires significant detective work that includes reading thousands of individual program, project, and award data contained within RAND's RaDiUS database or obtained from agency sources. The process for collecting data and the criteria for inclusion are presented here. Our findings are presented in Chapter Two.

---

[2]The case study described in the appendix sought to include all S&T activities without regard to R&D budgetary classification.

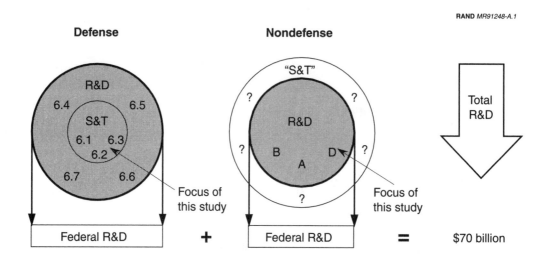

Figure A.1—"Research and Development" Versus "Science and Technology"

Sources of the Data

Figure A.2 shows the five steps taken to create the data for this inventory. Part one involved collecting data from official and primary data sources. A great deal of information on government R&D spending is electronically available through the RaDiUS database (http://radius.rand.org). RaDiUS is the first comprehensive, fully searchable data system that contains information on the approximately FY97 $72 billion of spending classified by the federal government as "research and development," as defined by OMB Circular A-11. RaDiUS contains information on federal government R&D activities derived from more than 500 different sources or budget or program data. RaDiUS is a full-text searchable database and records contain both budget and project information. We used this database in the first stage of data collection.

The RaDiUS database was searched using an iterative search strategy. Searches were conducted on words (such as "Germany" in conjunction with "collaboration") and on countries, regions, and international organizations (such as "Canada" or "European Union"). Dozens of searches were run to capture all relevant programs, projects, contracts, and other awards.

Part two involved examining and sorting the data and running additional searches where needed. Once the full set of relevant activities was identified, the project descriptions and award abstracts were sorted, coded, and classified according to the range of characteristics described below.

Part three of the process involved consultations with federal funding experts and with staff at the Office of Science and Technology Policy to identify where additional data were needed. We then contacted government officials to ask for assistance in

RAND*MR1248-A.2*

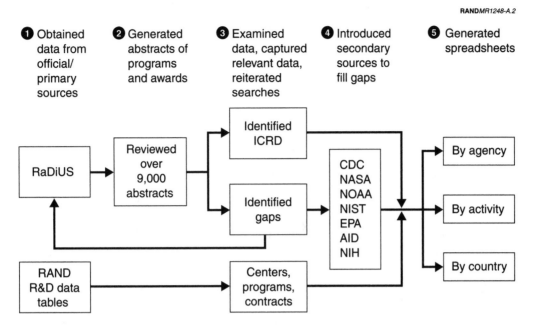

❶ Obtained data from official/ primary sources

❷ Generated abstracts of programs and awards

❸ Examined data, captured relevant data, reiterated searches

❹ Introduced secondary sources to fill gaps

❺ Generated spreadsheets

NOTES: CDC is Center for Disease Control; NASA is National Aeronautics and Space Administration; NOAA is National Oceanic and Atmospheric Administration; NIST is National Institute of Standards and Technology; EPA is Environmental Protection Agency; AID is Agency for International Development; and NIH is National Institutes of Health.

Figure A.2—Steps Taken to Create the Data Set

validating data obtained from RaDiUS and, if necessary, in identifying additional budget data. In some cases, supplementary data were not available from the agency.

Finally, the process involved compiling all the data collected from all sources, placing the data in spreadsheets, examining the data for duplications and obvious errors, and then analyzing the data set.

Criteria for Inclusion

Included in the final count was any type of program-based R&D activity—projects or awards (contract, grant, or cooperative agreement)—that had, as *one of its principal purposes*, the sponsorship of international cooperation with entities in other nations, including both groups and individuals working in the public, academic, or private sectors. Project descriptions that named a foreign collaborator and research subject were identified and categorized as formal, government-sponsored cooperation.

Clearly, much of the international activity, coordination, and sharing that goes on at an informal level was not captured by this inventory, since we limited the study to activities for which cooperation was a specific project goal. The focus of our collection efforts was on dollars spent on projects where cooperation was a specific aim of the R&D effort. Thus, the amount of funding identified in this inventory represents the baseline of activities in which the U.S. government was involved.

Where a project or award described international scientific or technical cooperation as a principal part of that activity, the *full average annual* budget authority for fiscal year 1997 was included in the inventory.[3] Among policy analysts examining scientific data, "whole counting" is a commonly-used methodology.[4] While this method may have led to overcounting in a limited number of cases, the alternatives were unworkable. Possible alternatives included (1) asking agency officials to report on the share of a project dedicated to R&D, a data point they usually do not have available; (2) contacting principal investigators directly and asking them to report on the extent of funding dedicated to ICRD, a herculean task given the final data set of nearly 5,300 projects; or (3) having RAND staff make a judgment, an impossible task without additional information.

Cooperation was defined for the purposes of this study as federally supported activities in which a U.S. government-funded researcher was involved in a project with a foreign researcher, a foreign research institution, a multinational institution, or a multinational research project. Projects and awards that fell within this definition encompassed scientist-to-scientist collaboration and field research in which a scientist worked with a collaborator to gain access to a natural resource; research for a Ph.D. dissertation when that activity was classified by the agency as "R&D"; and government agencies supporting the conduct of research through operational and technical support, again, where that activity was budgeted as R&D. The definition did not include activities for which a U.S. government official met briefly or shared data intermittently with counterparts from other countries—which would generally be considered "informal" cooperation.

Agencies that used contracts, grants, and cooperative agreements to conduct most or all of their research and development were the most fully represented in the RaDiUS database and therefore were the most fully represented in this inventory. When government money changes hands, records are made of the transactions, and the grant or contract recipient often provides a full description of the planned activities.[5] This is often referred to as extramural research. Agencies that primarily sponsor extramural research include the NSF,[6] HHS,[7] the USDA, and the nonlab-based activities of the DoD and DoE.

When the R&D is conducted within government laboratories—intramural research—spending is more difficult to track. Although we made an effort to identify and characterize these activities, cooperative activities in these parts of the government may not be fully represented in this study. Identifying and collecting information on intramural research involved, first, using RaDiUS to locate the likely federal agencies

---

[3]In many cases, the activities identified in this inventory were funded on a multiyear basis. In these cases, RaDiUS reports, and the project team counted, the average annual funding figure.

[4]Yoshiko Okubo, *Bibliometric Indicators and Analysis of Research Systems: Methods and Examples,* STI Working Papers 1997/1, OECD, Paris, 1997, p. 21.

[5]If international cooperation was established after the grant or contract was awarded, the activity will not be captured by this search methodology.

[6]Close to 95 percent of NSF R&D funds leave the agency in the form of grants or contracts.

[7]Close to 80 percent of HHS R&D funds leave the agency in the form of grants or contracts.

that contain these activities and, second, contacting the agencies to seek the information directly. Even though we made extensive efforts to contact agencies with program or lab-based activities, it was difficult at times to decouple the international activities from other activities going on in these agencies or laboratories. Agencies sponsoring this intramural activity included parts of NASA, the EPA, the NIST at the DoC, the DoD, the DoE, and the independent Smithsonian Institution.[8]

Coding the Data Set

To create a useful database for analysis, the data records were classified using four main categories:

- by region and by country, or, in cases where researchers from more than two nations were involved or where a U.S.-funded researcher reported working with a multinational research organization, as a "multinational" activity;

- by type of cooperation, in categories developed by RAND, for identifying the character of the cooperative projects or programs funded by the U.S. federal government (see Table A.1);

- by fields of science or technology, using a list adapted by RAND from the National Science Board list of areas of S&T (see Table A.2); and

- by sponsoring federal agency or independent group receiving a direct government R&D appropriation.

For example, a project with Mexico on the synthesis and characterization of solid "superacids" would be classified first as "Mexico," second as collaborative research because it involved scientist-to-scientist collaboration between a U.S. and a Mexican institution, third as "chemistry"—the area of science—and finally as a project being funded by the U.S. NSF. Similar classifications were made for all the projects identified in the database.

---

[8]The Smithsonian Institution is not a government agency. That institution, however, is unique in that it receives a direct line-item appropriation of R&D funds from the federal budget. These R&D funds are tracked and were considered in this study.

Table A.1

Types of Cooperative Activity Identified in the Course of the Study

Collaboration	A principal purpose of the research activity is to sponsor international collaboration of the following types: between a researcher funded by the U.S. government in a joint project with a collaborator from another country, when a researcher funded by the U.S. government is conducting a research program that involves actively sharing information with another researcher conducting the experimental or observational research, or when a researcher is contributing to an international cooperative project
Conference	Either foreign or domestic—including symposia, workshops, or other official meetings where scientists from around the world participate in a scientific or technical meeting to describe and share ongoing research
Database development	The U.S. government is sponsoring the creation of an international database of information being collected from sources worldwide, which will be available to researchers from around the world
Operational support	The U.S. government is funding the building, maintenance, and/or operation of an international research center designed specifically for the purposes of international collaboration in the United States or in a foreign country
Standards development	The U.S. government is sponsoring the development of a technical or scientific standard that will serve as the basis for future research, development, or production for practitioners around the world
Technology transfer	The U.S. government is actively seeking to transfer technology from a foreign country to the United States
Technical support	A U.S. government laboratory or a U.S. government-sponsored researcher is providing research and development results or other support to a foreign researcher or laboratory

Table A.2

Fields of Science Used to Identify the Nature of ICRD

Aeronautics & astronautics	Demography	Oceanography
Agricultural sciences	Earth sciences	Other earth sciences
Anthropology	Economics	Other engineering sciences
Archeology	Energy	Other life sciences
Atmospheric sciences	Environmental sciences	Other physical sciences
Biology		Other social sciences
Biomedical sciences	Geography	Physics
Biotechnology & genetics	Geology	Plant biology
Chemical engineering	Health	
Chemistry	Materials sciences	
Computer engineering	Mathematics	

INTERNATIONALIZATION OF SCIENTIFIC RESEARCH

Internationalization of scientific R&D is part of a trend transforming the face of science. The transformation is posing new challenges to priority setting among scientists and policymakers. The problem of adjudicating among competing priorities for scientific and technical investment—always a complex one—is made even more complex as the nature of new knowledge creation becomes collectivized and the locations at which these activities take place disperse globally.

It is a truism to say that science is an international activity, but in the past this has generally meant that scientific knowledge is freely shared and available to benefit humankind. Nevertheless, over the past 20 years, it appears that actual scientist-to-scientist collaboration is indeed increasing. One indicator of this is the total number of papers jointly authored by international colleagues. Figure B.1 illustrates the increase in the number of papers internationally coauthored from 17 percent of all papers in 1981 to 29 percent of all papers in 1995 published worldwide. The figure also shows the continuation of a trend towards jointly authored papers overall.

Internationalization of scientific research arises in part from the increasing scientific excellence emerging around the world. Most of the advanced industrialized countries have, over time, moved towards a mean of investing about 2 percent of gross domestic product in R&D. Figure B.2 shows the increase in shares of spending in some major Organization for Economic Cooperation and Development (OECD) economies, while other "big spenders" have tended to decrease the share of R&D towards the 2 percent mark. Moreover, in all the OECD countries, the number of researchers trained in science and/or technology has increased over the past 20 years.

Dispersed scientific excellence alone cannot account for the dramatic increase in the internationalization of scientific and technical research. International contacts, while stimulating, are more costly in terms of time and travel and more cumbersome in terms of cultural and language differences than connections within a single country. The increasing facility of communications and travel has also contributed to increased ties, but even here, it is difficult to say that this is a primary factor affecting internationalization. There may be changes in the manner in which science is conducted that are having an even more basic and fundamental influence on science.

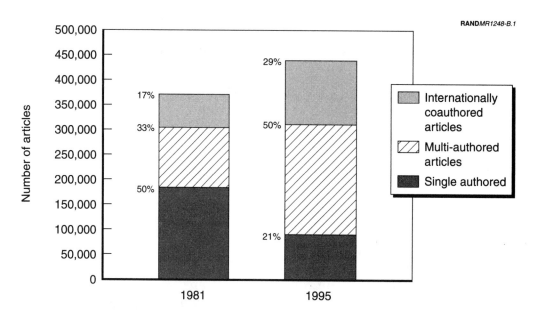

SOURCE: Appendix Table 5–53, *Science & Engineering Indicators 1998*, NSF.

Figure B.1—Internationally Coauthored Scientific and Technical Articles as a Share of All S&T

Some have suggested that the internationalization of S&T is the result of a radical structural transition to a more tightly organized, rationalized, and managed social institution. According to John Ziman, "knowledge creation is being collectivized."[1] And, even as Derek de Solla Price observed in the early 1960s that an increasing number of scientific papers were being coauthored, in the late 1990s he would note that an increasing number of papers are being *internationally* coauthored, as illustrated in Figure B.1. He might go on to add that the growth in scientific and technological output appears to engender teamwork in research, indicated by both increasing coauthorship as well as by the increasingly interdisciplinary nature of teams of researchers working on specific projects. As Ziman notes,

> The growth of team research in almost every field of science and technology is not due entirely to the increasing scale of research projects. The advance of knowledge has come to depend on the active collaboration of scientists with specialized skills drawn from a number of distinct areas or traditions.[2]

Michael Gibbons and colleagues have suggested that the collectivized, team-based approach to R&D is a new method of knowledge production resulting from the expansion in the supply of knowledge producers and the demand for specialized

---

[1]John Ziman, *Prometheus Bond*, UK: Cambridge University Press, 1994, p. viii.
[2]*Ibid.*, p. 60.

RAND *MR91248-B.2*

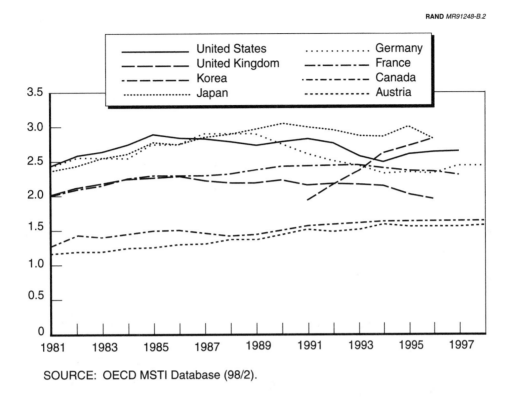

SOURCE: OECD MSTI Database (98/2).

Figure B.2—Gross Expenditure on R&D

knowledge. The increase in the number of scientists and scientific papers, as well a shift in the nature of the questions asked of science (moving from basic towards functional questions) at the end of the 20th century constitutes enough difference, according to Gibbons, to warrant a new name: "Mode 2" knowledge creation. The shifts in knowledge creation both result from and further encourage development of science as a truly international enterprise, organized systematically on a global scale.[3]

Mode 2 knowledge creation is not eliminating "Mode 1"—traditional disciplinary science. It is growing out of, emerging alongside, and augmenting Mode 1. It is one of the imperatives of Mode 2 that understanding new knowledge as it emerges requires participation in its generation. Thus, scientists are seeking to work together more often and across more disciplines than before.

> The goals of participation are no longer simply to secure national advantage, commercial or otherwise. Indeed, the very notion of what constitutes an economic benefit, and for whom, is at the root of many debates not only in environmental science but in biotechnology and the medical sciences as well.[4]

---

[3]Michael Gibbons et. al., *The New Production of Knowledge: The Dynamics of Science and Research in Contemporary Societies*, London: Sage Publications, 1994, p. 13.

[4]*Ibid.*, p. 15.

Indeed, John Ziman has suggested that the main effects of scientific and technological change in the 20th century have been to "hasten an overall trend from individual to collective modes of work."[5] In many fields of science, he says, it is becoming unusual, even for experienced researchers, to work on their own.[6] Certainly, the bibliometric data on coauthorships in Figure B.1 would seem to uphold this view.

"COLLECTIVIZING" SCIENCE

The collectivization of scientific research demonstrated by increasing coauthorship and team-based research (Figure B.1 shows the increase in the number of coauthored papers) has also led to the integration of the process of discovery with the application and use of that knowledge. The uses of knowledge, and the purpose to which new information is put, are increasingly part of the process of allocating funds and dispersing information. Some view the increasingly utilitarian nature of research with alarm, as an abandonment of basic knowledge creation.[7] However, the links between scientific question, theory, experiment, and purpose (the context of application) are a feature of "Mode 2" research—the dynamic, interdisciplinary, team-based form of knowledge creation. All manner of questions, from basic to applied, are included as part of a collectivized approach to science. Basic science has not been left behind, it has become part of a more accountable, integrated approach to research.

The fields of science that are leading the trend towards collectivization and internationalization are clinical medicine, physics, and biomedicine. These fields also lead the world in terms of number of papers published overall and number of internationally coauthored papers.[8] As illustrated in Figure B.3, the number of internationally coauthored articles in these fields have at least doubled between the early 1980s and the early 1990s. (By comparison, U.S. government funding has tended to favor earth and space sciences research, followed closely by physics and biomedicine.[9])

Research by Yoshiko Okubo and others shows that the advanced industrialized countries have been moving slowly away from investment in physics and chemistry—sciences that support a traditional industrial base—and more towards the life, environmental, and biological sciences.[10] Okubo has further discovered that collaborating countries tend to cluster into two different types: (1) countries collab-

---

[5]Ziman, p. 64.

[6]*Ibid.*, p. 64.

[7]Recent publications by the U.S. Council on Competitiveness (*The New Challenge to America's Prosperity: Findings from the Innovation Index*, 1999) and the National Academy of Sciences (*Capitalizing on Investments in Science and Technology*, 1999) cite a reduction in basic research as a significant weakness facing the U.S. innovation system.

[8]National Science Board, *Science and Engineering Indicators—1998*, Arlington, VA: The National Science Foundation, Table 5-51.

[9]Caroline Wagner, *International Cooperation in Research and Development*, RAND, MR-900-OSTP, 1997, p. 20.

[10]Y. Okubo et al., "Structure of International Collaboration Science: Typology of Countries Through Multivariate Techniques Using a Link Indicator," *Scientometrics*, Vol. 25, No. 2, 1992, p. 321–351.

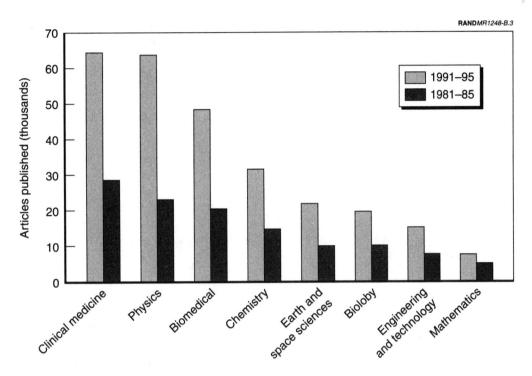

SOURCE: Appendix Table 5–53, *Science & Engineering Indicators 1998*, NSF

Figure B.3—Internationally Coauthored Articles by Field of Collaboration

orating mainly in physics, and (2) countries collaborating mainly in biology and/or clinical medicine. Countries collaborating in physics are predominantly Western and Eastern European countries. Countries occupying the biology/clinical medicine cluster are mostly in the Asia-Pacific region as well as Africa and South America.[11] Collaboration in biomedicine is more widely and evenly undertaken by more countries than other fields, while collaboration in physics, because of the scale of investment, tends to be concentrated in scientifically large countries.[12]

In terms of sheer numbers of papers coauthored internationally, the United States leads all other countries with more than twice the number of papers coauthored than the next largest country, Germany. Figures B.4 and B.5 show which countries are most actively publishing internationally and how this has changed since the early 1980s. Many countries have more than doubled the number of internationally coauthored papers.

The degree of internationalization of S&T in a country—the extent to which national scientists collaborate with foreign counterparts—does not track with the gross num-

---

[11]*Ibid.*, p. 333.

[12]*Ibid.*, p. 330.

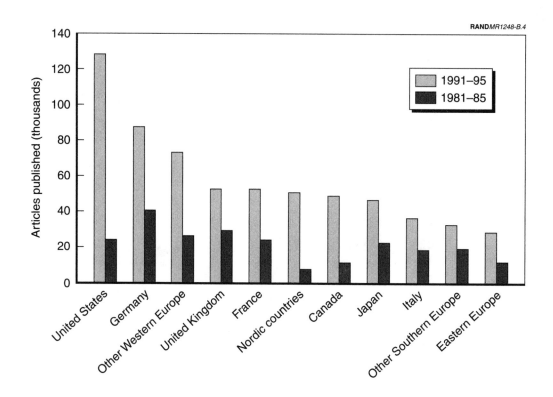

Figure B.4—Internationally Coauthored Articles by Country—1

ber of papers published. In fact, in terms of the *intensity* of international collaboration, the United States may be one of the least "internationalized" countries in the world.[13] Figure B.6 shows a wheel of countries from the least internationalized to the most internationalized, based on publications data, starting with the former Soviet Union, India, Japan, and the United States, to the most internationalized in the regions of South and Central America and in parts of Asia and the Pacific. The degree of internationalization is roughly inverse to the size of the scientific enterprise in a particular country, with larger countries being less likely than smaller countries to collaborate internationally.

The reasons for collaboration appear to include the level and interests of scientists in different countries, as well as historical political linkages such as those shared by the British Commonwealth countries. Sharing a common language can positively influence collaboration, as can geographic proximity. The top collaborator with the United States is Canada, in part because of geographic proximity but also because of

---

[13]The degree of internationalization is figured by comparing the share of all articles published to the total number of internationally coauthored articles published. The figure for the United States may not fully represent internationalization, since a number of foreign researchers reside in the United States and list their local address when publishing. Therefore, the U.S. data may understate the degree of internationalization.

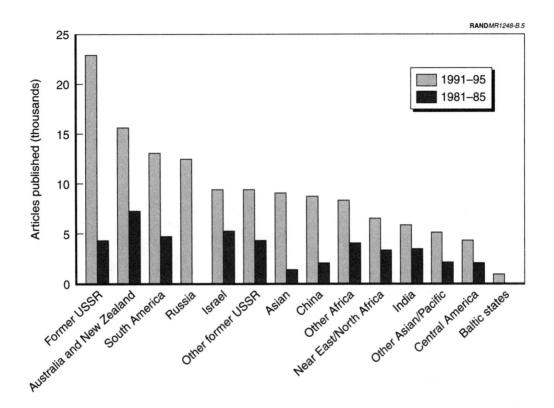

SOURCE: Appendix Table 4–48, *Science & Engineering Indicators 1998*, NSF.

Figure B.5—Internationally Coauthored Articles by Country—2

a shared culture, language, and common scientific problems (such as the environment). The Ukraine's top collaborator is Russia, and South Korea is much more likely to collaborate with Japan than with almost any other country except the United States. Spain is among Argentina's top three collaborating partners. New Zealand, Australia, and Singapore also form a geographic and cultural link that fosters close scientific ties.[14]

MOTIVATIONS FOR SCIENTIFIC COLLABORATION

There are a number of reasons why scientists choose to collaborate, and why government is interested in funding this collaboration. These include the following broad characterizations.[15]

---

[14]National Science Board, Table 5-54.

[15]These categories and examples were developed by Linda Staheli, Staheli and Associates, under contract to RAND.

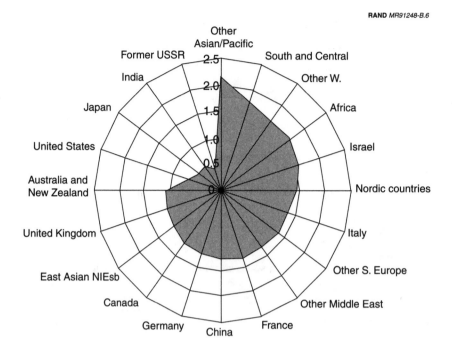

RAND *MR91248-B.6*

SOURCE: Annex Table 4.21, Science, Technology and Industry Outlook 1998, OECD.

Figure B.6—Degree of Internationalization

- The natural *curiosity* of scientists seeking to expand their knowledge base. Scientists have long sought to advance their knowledge base, collaborating with counterparts wherever they are geographically located. Principle funding agencies for this type of research in the U.S. government are the NSF and NIH. Examples of these types of projects include the multilaterally funded "Human Frontier Science Program" (HFSP)—a unique organization initiated by Japan in 1986 and funded by a handful of governments to support the neurosciences and basic molecular biology.

DATA TABLE

Table C.1

Breakdown of Agency Support for ICRD

Agency or Department	ICRD Spending Estimates, FY97 (US 000)	FY97 Total R&D Budget Authority (US 000)	ICRD Spending Estimates, FY95 (US 000)	FY95 Total R&D Budget Authority (US 000)
Agency for International Development	225,176	225,176	313,951	371,200
Department of Agriculture	10,219	1,377,228	7,525	1,375,000
Department of Commerce	41,466	915,485	4,167	1,183,000
Department of Defense	263,000	37,322,651	465,196	36,335,000
Department of Education	2,491	185,000	NA	169,000
Department of Energy	183,000	5,453,658	171,477	5,795,000
Environmental Protection Agency	21,000	539,000	26,117	584,000
Department of Health and Human Services	215,000	12,488,152	122,547	11,412,000
Department of the Interior	2,845	578,907	384	681,000
National Aeronautics and Space Administration	3,150,510	9,038,485	1,939,785	9,078,000
National Science Foundation	206,189	2,248,520	220,780	2,145,000
Smithsonian Institution*	31,900	137,000	29,150	132,000
Department of Transportation	1,299	612,189	NA	661,000
Department of Veterans Affairs	6,684	265,200	2,000	266,000
Other R&D spending	32,500		26,525	
TOTAL	4,393,279	71,386,651	3,329,604	70,187,200

* The Smithsonian is not a federal government agency, but it receives a direct R&D appropriation and so is included in this inventory.